DARKER SISTER

DARKER SISTER

A POETRY AND ESSAY
COLLECTION

Joiya Morrison-Efemini

Nymeria Publishing LLC

First published in the United States of America by
Nymeria Publishing LLC, 2021

Copyright © 2021 by Joiya Morrison-Efemini

Nymeria Publishing
PO Box 85981
Lexington, SC 29073
Visit our website at www.nymeriapublishing.com

ISBN 978-1-7363027-3-6

Printed in U.S.A

This book is dedicated to all my sisters and brothers who have been victims of State-sanctioned violence and murder. This book is dedicated to the fight against a system of white supremacy that perpetuates the belief that we don't matter. It is dedicated to the families of the fallen who have braved the denigration of their loved ones and fearlessly demanded justice.

BLACK LIVES MATTER.

POEMS

Two: Seated At The Table

Three: Take My Hand

Part One: Unmasked

We Wear the Mask

Paul Laurence Dunbar (1872-1906)

We wear the mask that grins and lies,
It hides our cheeks and shades our eyes,—
This debt we pay to human guile;
With torn and bleeding hearts we smile,
And mouth with myriad subtleties.

Why should the world be over-wise,
In counting all our tears and sighs?
Nay, let them only see us, while
We wear the mask.

We smile, but, O great Christ, our cries
To thee from tortured souls arise.
We sing, but oh the clay is vile
Beneath our feet, and long the mile;
But let the world dream otherwise,
We wear the mask!

Comfortable Walk

He is on his feet for twelve hours, at work. So, he called ahead, on the recommendation of a colleague. He wears a size thirteen. He can't just walk in and buy a pair of shoes. He lucked out. The outlet store had exactly the style, size and color he wanted. The associate he spoke with willingly reserved the pair for him on a twenty-four-hour hold. She was so accommodating.

We made it a family outing. We planned to browse the outlets the way we used to, before having our first baby, a boy; just a few months old. We went to that store first. So he could claim his shoes. We entered and I decided to peruse while he approached the register.

"I'm here to try on a pair of shoes. I called in and put them on hold."

"Name?" The twenty-something white female at the register looked innocent enough.

"Efemini. Starts with an E."

"Yes. Okay. I see." She looked through the boxes piled neatly on the shelf behind the register. The twenty-four-hour holds. For easy access.

"Well, I don't think you want these exact shoes."

She held the box close, the way I held our son.

"We have other styles, though. Cheaper." Her voice was saccharin.

"Why do I not want them?" He still didn't know where this was going. He didn't grow up here. My surroundings blurred. All I could see was my husband and my baby, and this pseudo-human.

"Well, they are mainly for people who spend a lot of time on their feet."

"I spend a lot of time on my feet."

"No, like," Extremely long pause. "Doctors."

"I am a doctor." There was a change in his voice. But I could tell from her face, she did not detect it. He couldn't be angry on top of being 6'2", male, and Black.

4

"Oh." Her eyes made a beeline to me. I stood behind him, but not directly. Her eyes prodded mine, and interrogated.

"Is he telling me the truth?" They asked.

My eyes invoked their right to remain silent, even though she was the one incriminating herself. They glared at her, grabbed her prods and jabbed back at her, electrified. I can be angry.

She turned her back to all of us and shuffled to the storeroom. Admonished.

She returned with the same box. His shoes.

He was already seated, waiting for her. I was next to him. Our infant son gurgled blissfully in my arms. He was not yet one. This was his first encounter. He would not retain it. For that day, at least, he could be an unknowing witness to a miniscule mind that couldn't see his Daddy for the champion he is.

No one smiled. She knelt. She opened the box. She

hesitated. He and I looked at one another, scoffing a cappella. He bent down to pick up his shoe. She stood, taking two steps back as he tried it on. Then the other. She took another step back when he stood to walk in them.

"Yeah. I mean, you're going to love them. You know, we all wear them here, since we're on our feet a lot too." It was then I looked at her feet. She wore the shoes she tried to talk him out of. The same style. The same color. Much smaller. Shoes reserved for doctors.

We shopped effusively that day. We entered the car at the end of it all, our arms sore from ripping one million invisible labels off our baby, ourselves, and one another.

WELL-MEANING

This is the free pass
you get
to assert
every
reckless
notion
wafting
through your mindless
ethos
and wisping
from your over
confident
mouth and I
am expected to
take it
as:
a compliment,
a joke,
constructive criticism,
the truth
even
if the truth kills,
a misunderstanding,
an opportunity
to teach you just how

your
tactless
good intentioned
porcupine
quills
bore
into my heart
notions like yours
murder
But,
after all
it's the intent that counts
and YOUR heart
is in the right place.
YOUR HEART is in the right place.
my heart is in my throat.

NOT EVEN BLACK

Speaking of your eldest daughter, you tell me how broken up she is, and before I can find comfort in your family's sympathy, you continue

...and she's not even Black...

Not even Black. As if, she gets super special kudos. She can be devastated by the murder of a person who does not look like her. *Isn't she great?*

I wonder how you would take it if I said, "It's just awful! My husband was so heartbroken over that rape and murder, and he's not even a woman." Or, "My son is so troubled by this history unit focusing on the Jewish Holocaust, and he's not even Jewish."

I would never say that. I would never even think it. I would never relate a brutality first to race, in rating the level of horrendousness, in assessing my degree of disgust and outrage, in determining my empathy.

You reminded me some people do. Some people can watch a video of a man being asphyxiated, or shot in the back while running away unarmed, or beaten to death. Be outraged. Be heartbroken. Be surprised. Even though he's Black.

HALLWAY

It was his
first week
of middle
school
6th grade
the big leagues.
He
asked for a bathroom pass
and on his
way back to the classroom,
He
was stopped
by an 8th grader
He
didn't know
had never seen
had to look up to
in baritone
"Hey, Kid!
Why are you guys so good at basketball?"
He
shrugged.
Not sure who "you guys" were
He
played soccer.

"'Cause all you have to be good at
is running, shooting, and stealing."
Sinister
Laughter
Condescension
followed
Him
to class,
beat
Him
through the door,
crammed in with
Him
at the desk
reverberated
over the teacher's lesson…

FALLACY

I know you think
Jesus
led you
to call me
with an offer
to endorse
my kids
to have a chat
with my brown babies
smile on them
testify
someone white
loves them and believes
their lives have value
but
My God
would never perpetuate
the fallacy
that white validation
reigns
supreme
And,
just for clarification
Jesus
is not white

OWNERSHIP

I chaperoned a school field trip with the third-grade class. My daughter and I were two of less than fifteen African Americans going on a trip with one hundred seventy students, eight teachers, and sixteen parent chaperones. When we boarded the bus, your daughter was so excited. Our bus was being driven by the African American driver who operated her regular route. She exclaimed, "Oh, he's mine! I own him!"

To which, I sternly corrected, "No, Kenzie, you do not."

"Yes, I do!" She insisted. "He's mine. I own him."

"We don't own people. You do not own that man."

"I do!" Her blue eyes bore into me. Her silky blonde hair bobbed with her insistence.

I did not say another word to her.

A few weeks later, when I saw you at the park with your kids, having just arrived with mine, I took you aside. I relayed the conversation to you, and there was a hint of amusement in your eyes. It didn't surprise me. You are also blue-eyed and

14

blonde. Your pronunciation sings the songs of the South.
And, as much as I would like to erase the stereotype from my
psyche, after twenty years of living in the South, you
reaffirmed for me; some Southerners willingly slaughter
ethics to protect their heritage of patriotic superiority.

"I'll have a talk with her," you said.

At a class party a few weeks later, she approached me
timidly and apologized for being disrespectful. "I forgive
you," I said to her, with a warm smile.

Later, as we passed out sweets to the children, you said, "I saw
Kenzie talking to you. I hope she apologized. My issue was
not with what she said so much as her blatant disrespect. She
knows better than to argue with adults."

I looked at you, choosing uncomfortable silence. I didn't
address your ignorance. I knew better than to argue with you.

UNNECESSARY

You called to chat
like we do now
because we can't hang out five days a week
at the gym anymore,
oblivious to the invisible
airborne
sputum of others,
possibly infected
and even though we have this pact of
joyful
solidarity
I could not shake my
malaise
What's wrong?
I'm stuck in a funk. I'm glued to the news. I can't stop watching
the coverage about Ahmaud Arbery.
Oh, I know. It was all so unnecessary.
Unnecessary.
Like when my kids take four
paper towels to dry their hands
or, when my dog barks viciously
at Amazon packages being dropped off
Is that what you think?
Those monsters overreacted to Ahmaud's daily run?

They went too far when they decided to hunt him?
a Black man
in their neighborhood
Things maybe just got out of hand
When he decided to fight
back instead of cowering?
Their perception of Ahmaud
and conclusions
about who he was
were exaggerated?
Maybe if they had approached
him calmly?
asked him questions?
had a nice talk
with him to find out
he was an
innocent
man
out for a run.

Their invisible
infected ideals
murdered a twenty-five-year-old man,
and you describe it as
something
simply
superfluous

JUSTIFIED

It's my understanding

you said, and immediately
my jaw locked
my stomach forced a handspring
images of my children leapt
from my heart
sailors
abandoning ship
I have no confidence
in your understanding

it's fear on fear
the police are just as scared
as your husband
and your son

For the sake of your argument,
I'll leave my husband out of it
You think he's a threat;
6'2"
bald
lithe and muscular
lean
his voice

a deep, wide bass drum
majestic
nutmeg skin
because centuries of dehumanization
have spilled into your eyes
your psyche sopped
it up
you don't even realize
you see him as a fraction of a man
exponentially more deadly
than if he shared your husband's
khaki
coloration

My eldest son is fifteen
6'
that same lithe,
muscular
thin
magnificence
as his Daddy
head full of golden locs
you probably characterize
as *dread*

He suckled at my breast
I wiped his butt
you are a mother too

My terrifying husband
and I must equip
this child
of ours
for his encounters
with police
jaywalking
driving to
driving from
riding his scooter
out for a run
walking
buying skittles

show them you are human
tell them you attend Pope HS
you play varsity soccer
your dad is a doctor
your mom is a lawyer
but don't tell them your mom is a lawyer first
or they might think you're threatening them
maintain eye contact
have a neutral face
speak clearly, but not loudly
move slowly
don't ever
ever
ever

ever
ever run,
don't
ever
run
not ever

We know you see men and boys
women
children like you
suffering
execution
absent judge
vacant jury
We know you will be terrified
Of being killed
without cause,
But, please,
Baby
Do not run!
ever

Realize this!
Is it unconscionable to you?

If the police officers are just as afraid of him
as he is of them
when he's running away

If they are no longer in danger
of being harmed
by my unarmed
fifteen-year-old
son
running away

Why do I have to be petrified
of him
as he's
being shot in the back?

REACHING OUT

We volunteer at the school together
we smile
exchange pleasantries
We live less than a mile from one another
but you have never been in my house
and I haven't been in yours
I don't have your cell number
you don't have mine
but Facebook says we are
friends.
Once, at a birthday party
both of our children
were invited to,
we talked for two hours straight,
just the two of us,
and I remember thinking how delightful you are.
Nearly a year has passed…
and the news won't stop showing
brown folks being executed
Yesterday you sent me a private message
via Facebook
Hi. God has been putting you on my heart big time!
If you ever want to walk the dogs or talk let me know! XO
I wish I could be honest with you and tell you
reaching out to me
in that way

made my heart heavier
with the weight of not knowing
how to respond
because you have never been a person
I have gone to
when I needed to talk
the murder of my unarmed sisters and brothers
wouldn't cause me to start
I am not someone you run to
bleeding heart
in your hands
we are only friends
on the face
of a social media platform
I cannot be honest with you
without sounding
unfriendly
I respond
Thank you for thinking of me
YOU AGAIN
I'm praying for you. See you soon.
And, I pray for a little time
before you do.

PROTEST

We volunteer at the school together
smile
exchange pleasantries
We live in the same town,
our kids go to the same schools
you have never been in my house
and I haven't been in yours
I don't have your cell number
and you don't have mine
but Facebook says we are
friends
you are an amazing artist
we chatted a good bit about your work
and how you were discovered on Instagram
how people see God in your art
in ways that dazzle you
you glorify God
and God rained favor
you encouraged me
to use social media too
for my writing

I haven't seen
you in person in over a year
then
you show up next to me,

out protesting with my family,
I don't recognize you at first –
these masks we all wear
but your voice is familiar
you see us
from your car
driving by
my son, T,
first and then me

you pull over
park
get out
grab the sign you used a few days before
at a different protest

you join us

your life imitating
your art

I stand with you
you say,
and I feel like an image
on one of your canvases

STAR WARS

two
mothers
same church
both with Star Wars
loving sons
when you came over for coffee
your son had already seen
the newest installation
I asked
how he liked it
assuming I already knew
you answered with
small talk
I have to tell
you he was just really
so disappointed
with the forced diversity
you know
he didn't think it was appropriate
you know
in keeping with the overall theme
of the movies
they have always
been erstwhile tales
Blacks and women and Asians
in leading roles

just wasn't
historically accurate
you know

I elucidated:
Hmmm….
It's funny
he sees Star Wars
as historical
what, with the flying cars and all
our family likes to think of it as futuristic
and wouldn't it be lovely if
Star Wars is a forecast of what our future will be,
diversity
not forced
not resented
but aspired to
by all

I thought:
Big Talk
From your white son
who gets
a two-hour glimpse
into being
underrepresented
in film
and

has the audacity to
notice
and complain.

and you, my Christian sister
lacking the wisdom
to check
his privilege.

NICOLE, YOU'RE BLACK

My younger sister's
welcome to kindergarten
was a wooden cubby with a hook
for her bookbag
and her shoes
during circle time
a metal lunch box like her Big Sissy
and a thermos for soup
an amiable teacher
and a classmate
who
every single day for two weeks
insisted on reminding her
several times a day,
Nicole, you're Black.

In second grade
when a golden boy
called her
NIGGER
She reported him
But the teacher shrugged
Well, now you see how name calling
feels.
I overheard you and some other girls

saying someone had cooties.

When she told our parents
they handled it
administration put a stop
to the full slur

The boy resorted to calling her a
NIG
What?
I'm not saying the whole word!

LETTER TO AMY COOPER

Dear Amy,
You are not used to
being told what to do
especially by a Black man
and when one
was so bold
as to remind you of the rules
you tried to have him killed
YOU KNOW
what happens
when white women
call the police
on Black men
Why else did you threaten him
first
and then
change your voice
from terroristic
to terrified?

MISTAKEN IDENTITY

I'm standing in line to register my boys for club soccer. The only brown skin in the room. I'm fourth or fifth in line. There is only one line. There are three busy white women at a foldable table up front; smiling, chatting, shuffling papers and helping the first white man in line. One of the women looks up, scans the line, locks eyes with me. She classifies me, grabs a clipboard officiously, locks a stack of papers in place on it, and walks authoritatively toward me.

"Come with me, and we'll get you all squared away." Her mouth shows teeth.

"Oh, thank you," I say. "But they were first." I know how these situations can go. A week ago at tryouts, two dads frowned at me and spoke furiously to one another for an hour before the angriest one approached me.

"Nice that your son can just walk out here and take a spot on the team. Our boys have played for this club for years." His face was red and he had a small spit bubble in the corner of his mouth.

"I guess it's just like everything else in life." I shrugged, smiled. "Nothing is guaranteed."

That was our club soccer welcome. Our sons had always played recreationally. But, we recognized they needed to be more competitive. We left on day one with an offer, while that angry dad's son dragged his cleats through the gravel parking lot, his spot still uncertain.

I do not see them here today; those entitled fathers.

"Yes, but you need to apply for the scholarship, correct?" I recognize now the same condescension from last week.

Last month.

Last year.

So many ex conversations.

But this will not be the last.

"Scholarship?"

"Yes. There's separate paperwork for that. It can seem complicated. Come with me. I will walk you through it." She puts her hand on my elbow to guide me.

"Is the scholarship merit-based?" I ask, hoping. Maybe my sons' extraordinary talent has preceded me.

"No. It's need-based. It's financial aid." Her volume increases with each syllable. She is speaking to me slowly, as if English is not my native tongue.

I can see the people around me shift closer, not wanting to miss a word of the spectacle. Their ears stretch but their eyes do not engage.

"I don't think we'll qualify," I say, almost whispering. "My husband and I." I add, reaching out for his support. I want her to know it's there.

"Are you sure? It won't hurt to try. Club soccer is so expensive!" She gives me an encouraging wink.

"I'm sure." I connect my irises with hers, now. "My husband is a physician. And, I'm an attorney. We don't qualify."

I speak to her the same way she has spoken to me; too many decibels for this space, with perfect diction, pronouncing each word as if she is a new speaker of English, and somewhat dull.

Her face turns as red as the father's from last week. She stutters something quietly, more quietly than she has spoken anything to me in this entire interaction.

"Excuse me?" I demand. Another decibel added. I want everyone to hear this.

"I'm sorry." Her voice still soft. "I have mistaken you for someone I spoke to on the phone earlier."

"Huh." I reverse the shame. "Was it a video call? Did she look like me?"

There is no answer. I look to the man in front of me, and the woman in front of him, who have both stopped pretending to be disinterested, and are now staring. At me. Foolishly, I am expecting to see substantiation on their faces. Shame on me. Instead, I see their eyes lift up the white woman who humiliated me. She is now, hunched over, shrunken down to actual size. They feel sorry for her.

My Black back is so straight; they have mistaken my defensive stance and taken offense.

DEAR TEACHER,

When my son had a serious
falling out
with a classmate
and stormed out
of your classroom,
slamming the door
behind him
it was absolutely unacceptable
we reprimanded him at home
he deserved consequences

but,

NO
he did not require
Tier 2 behavior management,
as you recommended

You knew
those two boys had issues
boiling
from the beginning of the school year
you chose
not to deescalate
continuously
taking the lighter child's side
or simply looking away

my son complained of that boy
here at home
we encouraged him to walk away
you
never alerted
us of the problem

My child was wrong.

His wrong did not warrant
a recorded
infraction
following him
for eight years

as you suggested
I
brought in the principal
because
my son had never
been in trouble
for anything
ever
in school in the five years he'd been there
until that incident
in your classroom

The principal agreed with me

The next year,
at a parent teacher conference,
with the next teacher,
we were told how
delightful
bright
participative
witty
helpful
generous
too chatty
our son was
and,
to her surprise,
impulsive
(calling out without raising his hand)
but not violent

You cautioned her
off the record
our son
was
violent
because you'd failed at stamping
it in writing

Violent?

For arguing with a peer
and slamming a door
in fourth grade

Violent!

I said nothing
then
because he'd acquitted
himself

He had a teacher
who could
incentivize
correct
evaluate
laugh with him
tolerate his age-appropriate
behavior
recognize him as
beautiful,
even in brown

I learned
you made a statement to your class
the next year
rebuking Colin Kaepernick
for taking a knee,

demoralizing the hero
of a child
in your class

And my next child
told me
once
she sat
chocolate,
in a sea of vanilla,
you observed the group,
all
playing with flashlights
stormed up to her
singled her out
demanding she
stop
playing
with her flashlight
turned your back
and retreated
while the other children continued
playing with theirs

I had planned
to remain silent
because my child
your student

had acquitted himself

Your
tainted dart
missed its mark,

I thought

Now I see your quiver
is fully stocked

you have access to
too many brown children

Saying nothing,
I am complicit
when the brown
students you target
storm away from your attacks
feeling the need
to slam doors,
to shield themselves

I am complicit
when you succeed
in wrongfully convicting
every darker child
in your care

So, I must come for you.
I'm coming.

SWIMMING POOL

Then, we still had just three kids, under six. We were new to the neighborhood. We moved in before the school year ended, and kept you, a kindergartener, at your old school, for continuity. Do you remember how early we had to get up and how far we had to drive to get you to school every morning? You used to hold your baby sister for me while I showered, and somehow you always got her to sleep. You have always been a baby

whisperer.

On the first day of summer break, I packed everyone up along with lunch, snacks, and pool toys. We headed to the pool early, before the baby's naptime.

We parked in the lot and I was relieved there was only one other car there. I would be able to keep an eye on all three of you well. The lifeguard wouldn't report for a few more hours. Even then, I wouldn't totally take my eyes off you for long. We picked a table in the corner, in the shade. The other family had taken the other corner table, and were already in the pool – two kids older than the three of you, with what looked to be grandparents. You boys barely stood still for sunscreen, jumping from one foot to the other ready to dive in.

I stayed with the baby at the one-foot pool, positioning myself well, to keep an eye on her and you daredevil boys, just in case.

It was a new pool, and you both knew how to swim, but your brother was more cautious. He stayed on the shallow side, dog paddling with floaties on his arms and a big grin on his face, or hanging on to the wall. His goggles made him look like a giant mantis. Not you. You jumped in feet first from the side of the pool, your new favorite thing. I watched you swim to the ladder, knowing you were going to jump in over and over, and barely swim. Just then, your sister, who had been mostly toddling around the pool, slipped in, startling herself. I reached, pulled her up and into me, soothed her. Told her she was okay.

It was no more than a minute. When I glanced back over toward the two of you, the grandmother held you up by your hands - like you were rotten, reeking; like she knew your rank - her arms outstretched. There is a look of disgust on her face. "You weren't watching." She says, nearly dropping you down in front of me. "He nearly drowned. He shouldn't be in the deep end."

I looked at your face, anxiously mortified.

"Are you okay?" I asked you.

You nodded. It was not the time for me to encourage you to speak instead of nodding, as I usually would.

"He can swim." I said to her.

"He's struggling…."

"Look at me," I said. And, you looked up. "You have every right to be here. Just as much as everyone else who pays to be here, like we did. You can swim. You are a very strong swimmer."

And then to her.

"My sons can swim. Please do not put your hands on them

46

again."

She huffed away.

You ran past her right back to the deepest end. You jumped from the diving board and swam toward the ladder.

I watched. I grabbed your sister's floatie and slowly made my way to you.

The grandfather was in the deepest end with the two children, his back to me. You were swimming near them. The grandmother was sitting with her feet in the pool, facing me. I walked toward all of you and I could hear the grandfather talking, but I didn't hear what he was saying. Not at first. The grandmother began to shake her head "no" frantically, but the grandfather was not looking at her. He was looking at you. He was chiding you.

"Get out. You don't belong in here. Just get out."

This seventy-something white man was not chastened by the defeated look in your eyes; the confusion. He was not moved to tears by your round, brown, rising first grade face.

He must have finally made eye contact with his wife because

he finally shut up. Too cowardly to turn. To look at me. I wanted to kick him in the back of the head.

"Great job!" I said to you, shining my proudest smile; my bravest smile; my most bold smile. "You look absolutely olympic out there!"

Your trust in me canopied your head, protecting you from the words he vomited. Your smile mirrored mine.

They exited the pool then, from the ladder on the other side, far from me. They packed up as their grandkids whined and stomped their feet. They weren't ready to go.

I got in the pool with your sister, in her floaty, and swam over to you. I left her with you, further proof. You are capable. I swam over to your brother, took his hand, coaxed him over to you others.

We were in a circle, floating and splashing. kicking our feet. They left the pool to the sound of your giggles, my laughter, splashing.

I enjoyed the idea of them hearing us over the cries of their grandchildren; even over their car engine.

Part Two: Seated At The Table

I, Too
Langston Hughes (1901 – 1967)
I, too, sing America.

I am the darker brother.
They send me to eat in the kitchen
When company comes,
But I laugh,
And eat well,
And grow strong.

Tomorrow,
I'll be at the table
When company comes.
Nobody'll dare
Say to me
"Eat in the kitchen,"
Then.

Besides,
They'll see how beautiful I am
And be ashamed-

I, too, am America.

NIGERIAN; IN AMERICA

A Nigerian
immigrant,
armed
with a medical license
flippantly remarks
that systematic
racism
is just an excuse
for lazy
Blacks
to sit around
unemployed
sponge
off the system
loiter
steal
angry for no reason

on his first day
he enters a patient's room
all teeth and cheekbones
he opens wide to speak
No! Get out, Nigger!
the patient shouts
I demand a real doctor!
another doctor is called

in the cafeteria line,
he overhears a colleague
blast
...another dumb Black patient...

a nurse becomes adversarial
with him regarding an order for a patient
she attacks his credentials

a white woman
victimizes him in the elevator,
clutching her purse
and turning herself away
when he enters

an ultrasound tech
at least ten years his junior
marvels
You are so articulate!
her chin jutting forward
offering
the smile
of a benefactress

the only other brown faces he sees
clean
and cook

a janitor launches a power nod
his way;
the encouragement of a compatriot

a server in the cafeteria
lifts an earthen right hand
to pat her heart
he can feel the salutation of a mother
closing his day
fortifying him for those to come

the blue lights target him
two minutes from his house

suddenly
he understands
the white coat hanging
on the hook
behind him
is not bulletproof

he is asked whose car he is driving
he is asked to step out of the car
he is shoved against the car
backwards
handcuffed
held in place with a firm hand
pushing his neck

and shoulder down

he thinks the officer is trying to meld
his body and the car
he has no intention of moving

his right brake light is not working
he is told
thirty minutes later
after two more cars
with four more cops
arrive

when the handcuffs are removed
he is ordered to have a nice day

when he arrives at home
spent
his wife is cooking dinner
he asks her
quietly
to come outside
he asks her to enter the car
he asks her to engage the brake
he stands behind his car
the light illuminates

During dinner

he can't stop staring at his
infant son
asleep in a swing,

just feet away
his son is just like him
he can't help but to fear for him

He goes to bed four hundred years
wiser
on day one

COACH

he is eight
so when he tells you his name
and you ask him
Can I just call you _____ ?
your suggestion is not a nickname,
given affectionately
with familiarity,
your suggestion is an evasion
your rendering
sends a message to my son
and to the other children surrounding him
you all white
it is not necessary
for any of you
to learn his given name
his name is *too hard*
for you
and, he is not important enough
for you
to even give it a try

you didn't even try

for weeks you will ask my son
to dribble faster
run harder

kick stronger
than the competition

you will tell him not to ever give up

all the while he will be thinking
Coach, you did.

I tell my son
You Can Do Hard Things
he is eight
and he can pronounce his name
so why can't you
even
try?

SINGLE *black* FEMALE

We are in the grocery store, you and I, assessing meat
during a pandemic. Keeping our distance, wearing our masks.
But, also both intent on friendliness. I smile and wonder if
you will know I am smiling. I can tell from your voice you are
smiling back.

"Buy one, get one," you say to me. Your fair finger
pointing to chicken breasts, just a few shades lighter.

"Oh, nice!" I wait politely for you to finish choosing.

"Yeah, I usually cook one and freeze one." You advise.

"I wish," I laugh. "I have two teenagers at home!"

"Yeah. I know exactly what it is to be a single parent,"
you say. Then you proceed to tell me about your ex-wife. Her
drug addiction wreaked havoc on your family. You had to
eventually keep her away from your
growing boys. How you raised them alone and now they are
both off, college educated, successful white men. There is a
half-hearted, "You can do it too," in your voice. You accept

the burden of being my cheerleader.

My attention is bisected. First, I look down at my smooth umber hands to make sure I am wearing my engagement and wedding rings. They are beautiful. Upgraded on our tenth anniversary. Ornate. Impossible to miss, if you care to glance. You do not. You already know I must be single. I let you finish your tale of woe about a partner lost, a family neglected, abandoned. A saga of drug addiction.

When you finish, I ask you, "What is it about me that makes you assume I'm single?"

You stutter through a response. Your confidently crisp words withdraw, wilted. You glance down, finally. Spot my gorgeous rings. I smile curtly and walk away. My mask repositioned.

PROFESSION

My friend
was visiting her mother
at a rehab center
several weeks after
a devastating stroke
My friend wore scrubs
the nurse
her mother's nurse
asked
"What do you do?"
"I'm a dentist," my friend exposed
pearly whites.
"You mean a dental hygienist?" The nurse drilled.
"No." My friend blinked,
said a short prayer
for the pain-relieving gas of grace
like nitrous oxide
to fill the cavity
bore
she would need more fingers
on more hands
to count the number of times
she's had to shield
her
profession
her smile

fighting
decay
"I am a dentist."

EDUCATION

Social media abounds with the posts
by my white
friends
who say
they are
listening
and learning
Now.
The first Black people
were shackled
to this country in
1619
Virginia.
Four hundred and one years
and
hundreds of thousands
of Black bodies
strung up on trees
shot
asphyxiated
brutalized
split apart
violated
maimed
demoralized...
Now.

And with a straight face, you ask me
to teach you.
Teach you what, exactly?

I am a Black woman.
but
how can I speak for all
Black
women?
people?
Just as nuanced as you are,
WE ARE
You do not see
US
Millions of white images
are written
heroically
into books
and uplifting
movie scripts
smiling
on television commercials
being productive
in news
clips

My perception of white people
comes from 43 years

of interaction and relationship
with innumerable white people.
So I do not have a perception of
white people.
I can say, "Some white people..."
most
of the time
the words that follow
could apply to any person
of any race.
When God made me,
He made me
just like you,
and then obliterated the mold
even the most
honest
vulnerable
conversations with
only me
will not give you the education
you say you crave
I have seen your bookshelves
stocked with cookbooks,
parenting books,
books on Christianity,
bestselling novels
about the Jewish Holocaust
and the Great Depression,

about Women's Suffrage
all of your interests
standing in line,
proud
and useful.
Enlightenment into
the African experience
here in America
does not deserve your
time
money
or
prideful display.
You prefer it
secretly
over a lunch you pay for,
spoon-fed
and
unbound

BLACK HAIR

PART 1:
Running late for our gathering,

I snapped a picture

Of my daughter's loose hair,

a thick, coily jumble of

darkest brown locs,

With the caption:

Have my hands full. Will be there soon.

You replied with an exasperated emoji:

Oh my gosh! I feel so bad for you. I would not want to have my

fingers in that!

Did you know this was my daughter's crown?

I didn't send you this picture for your pity. Despite what you might

think, I'm teaching my daughter to be proud of her hair. And, she

should be proud. I shouldn't have to teach her this, but ignorant

statements like yours are constantly undermining the truth – our

hair is a bountiful gift from God.

PART 2:

At the pool, when a friend comments on the strength in my daughter's stroke and says swimming might be her sport, I reply she's a gymnast, and anyway, I would never encourage her to pick up swimming as her main sport because of the toll the chemicals take on her hair. That friend laughed out loud. "Certainly there are things you can put in it to protect it? You wouldn't discourage her just because of hair?"

I don't recall the rest of the conversation, but I do recall regret followed me for at least a week. I composed several responses to her dismissal, in my head.

I thought about how another friend's white daughter cannot swim in chlorine, only salt water, because of a skin condition. Does anyone question her mother's love, or her care for her child's skin when she limits swimming pool time? Would anyone laugh at her? Suggest she find some magic potion to protect the child's skin and continue dipping her daughter in the poison harming her because she's really good at swimming?

And, how is it that a white woman presumes to know more
than me about my Black daughter's hair or the Black hair care
industry.

"Just go find something."

She proposes.

PART 3:
I arrive to pick up my daughter
from Christian preschool
and both
teacher
and teacher's aide
stand by the door
the whole
class in a single file,
waiting
and both
teacher
and teacher's aide
on either side of my daughter
petting her
free
flexible
compact
corkscrews
when they spot me,

they turn into cheshire cats
We just love her hair.
It's so soft!
I smile.
Yes.
Like lamb's wool.
Like Jesus'
I paralyze them
all four
hands stand
still
both mouths stuck
ajar

I pray their ears are too
I tell them.
Please do not pet my child again.
She is not an animal.

Oh! No! We…we're…we wouldn't…

Do you pet the hair of your other students?
I demand.
No?
I answer for them.
Then, please, do not pet hers

KILLING CONFEDERATES

African Proverb: Until the story of the hunt is told by the Lion, the tale of the hunt will always glorify the hunter.

"How was the field trip?" I asked my youngest son, excitedly.

"Great." Sarcasm. "I killed a Confederate soldier."

"You what?"

"Yeah. We were each assigned a role – Confederate or Union soldier.

I got Confederate.

Our job was to go through all the dangers and obstacles soldiers faced during the Civil War.

We had to try to keep our soldiers alive.

Overcome the obstacles.

But, like, why would I try to keep a Confederate soldier alive?

He would have wanted me enslaved.

He wouldn't have even thought I was a person.

So, I killed him as fast as I could.

Then I had to sit out and watch

everyone else

try to survive."

Only in America are the losers

glorified

In the South, the Confederates

are heroes.

Their daughters

weep
for them still,
romanticizing their gallantry
raising money to erect
memorials
Their sons fly flags from pick up
trucks and general stores,
littering the region
with legacy
proudly
grandstanding
to the descendants of Africans
enslaved;
the Confederacy
was on the right
side of history

Picture
generations of daughters
of The Third Reich
weeping
at the immortal
impressions of their fallen

Picture
The Nazi Pride
Museum of Germany
a dazzling Imperial Eagle

at the entrance
swastikas
ubiquitous
Nazi soldiers hailed
as heroes,
statues of Hitler
and his colonels
preserved
beloved.

A Jewish child going there on a field trip
and being drafted
'Pretend to be a Nazi soldier,' they say to the Jewish child
'And try to keep him alive.'
Or, just think about that sweet
Jewish child,
riding in a car with his parents,
music trilling,
wind in his hair
free,
spotting
a Nazi flag,
in front of an ordinary looking house,
blowing proudly
in the same
wind
breezing
through his hair.

COLORBLIND

When I hear you say
I don't see color

I first think
of sunsets
tinged
with coral and periwinkle
Caribbean seas
turquoise and celadon
tigers
so orange
my tongue prickles
robin's eggs
in nests all over my back yard
in late spring
and early summer
the royal purple frock
of an iris

God's Masterstrokes

my
velvet
medium
chestnut
skin

is not on my mind
like it is on yours

at first

I snap out of it

I think you mean to say
you don't
think less of me
as society would like
for you,
a "white" person,
to
because I
display a darker hue

I wish you would say that

When you pretend you don't see my color,
it makes me wonder
if you think
denying
it protects me from
the images
it evokes,
fabricated
generations ago

by people who looked like you
perpetuated still

negro-nigger-black
black _____
cats
magic
mail
sites
market
list
eye
sheep
ball
mark

even in the thesaurus
threatening
equals
black

they
called us
black
when we weren't
black
at all

we still
are not
then they pretended
to be white
when they were its antithesis

I wish you would see
elasticity
my rich
pigment
survives

       slavery
       massacre
       Jim Crow
       segregation
       defaulted reparations

selfless restraint
       your babies
       chugged our vivacious balm
       we didn't kill them while we watched you kill ours,
       steal them
       all we could offer
       any child
       ever
       was stolen tears

pride
       we stand

fists up
shake misrepresentations off our shoulders

ageless beauty
      athleticism
            intelligence
                  ingenuity
                        traffic light
                        mop
                        refrigerated truck
                        automatic elevator doors
                        carbon light bulb filament
                        home security
                        hair brush
                        3D movies
                        too many to list
I bet you didn't know

If you would see me
If they would see us
treat us like a subject
in school
instead of a month-long
favor
if movies about us
just told the truth

It has a monologue all its own

Joiya Morrison-Efemini

You wouldn't have to try to overlook me

Such a hard role
to rewrite
the fictional
Black
in your history

INDEPENDENCE

My ancestors were not free
on July 4, 1776
when
the British were evicted
because the colonists didn't want
to donate
anymore
of their hard
earned
money

When the Founding Fathers
of the United States
drafted the remarkable
Constitution,
this more perfect union
declared all men equal
created by God
acknowledged inalienable rights
      my ancestors
      were only 3/5 human

Twelve
US Presidents
George Washington
Thomas Jefferson

James Madison
James Monroe
Andrew Jackson
Martin Van Buren
William Henry Harrison
John Tyler
James K. Polk
Zachary Taylor
Andrew Jackson
Ulysses S. Grant
owned
people

8 of them owned
souls
while serving
as President
of these
free
united
states

the fireworks are glorious
the day off
welcomed
the barbeques delicious
way too much alcohol
all

steeped in a tradition
of cruelly
fought
individuality
commenced
while my ancestors were still chattel
no days off
the only thing barbequed
back then was them
not welcome
brutalized
into framing
The White House
The US Capital
and the Statue of
Freedom
atop
Wall Street
Faneuil Hall
AKA the cradle
of liberty
Fort Sumpter
Monticello –
home of the man who made a declaration
of independence
KKK
forbidden from reading
indicted for writing

but they constructed
Harvard
Columbia
Princeton
Yale

Unwelcomed

Juneteenth,
June 19, 1865
89 years after America
became "beautiful"
the last known enslaved
were finally informed
Emancipation
Proclamation
enacted 2.5 years
before

because the original messenger was killed?
or because the owners of enslaved people
wanted one more free
harvest?
or because they were planning to keep us bound
for eternity?
some weren't
still aren't
interested

in making
an honest
living

MAN OF THE HOUSE

When one too many
salesmen
trespassed
upon my dad
in
His
upper
middle-class yard
weeding
or trimming
His
lilacs
or mowing
His
lawn
and asked,
Is the MAN
of the house at home?
Dad
smiled.
Just a moment.
ambled to
His
front door
and lawfully entered
His

home
He
shut the door behind
Him,
washed
His
hands and splashed
His
face
He
grabbed a paper towel
and a glass of ice water
He
savored
every last drop
and by the time
He
strutted
back to the front door
The salesman
was standing on the porch,
indignant
expectant
perplexed
as to why
the help
hadn't alerted
the homeowner

of his presence
and gradually realizing
troubled
he was looking at
exactly
who he had been looking for
Dad
grinned,
We don't want what you're peddling here.

UNSEEN

Usually I request the gym equipment
but
a lesson in independence,
I urge him to stand in line
himself
at twelve
to ask for a basketball
I watch him from the
treadmills
as he waits patiently
and
she
helps every single person in line
except for him
even the elderly
white gentlemen who approaches
her
after my son,
and then
she turns her back
to him
I walk up
furiously stand beside him
and still
she works diligently

ignoring us
Excuse me!
Yes?
Her bright teeth
Her generous smile
deceives her
narrow-minded
eyes
My son has been standing here for nearly ten minutes
waiting to be helped,
I lay my hand across his shoulders,
protectively.

Oh. I didn't even see him.
She looks at him now,
indifferent

Yes. I know.

CULTURAL CONFIDENCE

On another continent
she was born
into dulcet dialect
restorative dance
piquant cuisine
embellished dress
a native account

her world
homogenous with opportunity

She emigrated

when someone presumed white
tries to depreciate her
endowment
she lifts a mirrored shield
spectator to their suicide

She walks away intact

my cradle was haunted
by memory
of graves
I nursed
milk tainted

with dirty orts
slop scarcely
satisfying
mother tongue cut out
garments worn to shreds
bloodied

I was stolen
so, my mirror is dysmorphic

when someone presumed white
tries to depreciate me
I must first underline
my shield
I hold it upright
demanding it not be invisible
to their naked eye

they get to choose

tiny cells of me
shed
like dead skin
in our wake

PLEASE REMAIN SEATED

I will never again stand for the National Anthem.

Or maybe I will stand again when you say you can see.

Did you know during the War of 1812, when your Star-Spangled Banner was written, the enslaved were still shackled to this country?

Did you know many fled their bondage and allied themselves with the British? The British promised freedom, so enslaved runaways provided strategic intelligence, gave them access to supplies, and labored for them. Regiments of Black marines served under white British officers.

You take offense when the descendants of those warriors protest the anthem which sings, "No refuge could save the hireling and slave from the terror of flight, or the gloom of the grave." Check it for yourself - verse three.

A threat embedded in the lyrics

your beloved Francis Scott Key penned;

fantasizing the deaths of my enslaved ancestors.

Did you know?

You want us to stand and to hold our hearts and to sing a
song that threatens to kill us while day after day we watch
videos of overseers intoning that refrain.

You see us remain seated.
You see us kneel.
We hang our flags
upside down or not at all.
All you can think is,
disrespect

And you are threatened

by our refusal to accept extermination
You are threatened
when we refuse to stand for a country
standing for
only you

BLACK REPRESENTATIVE

Seven teenage friends
sitting around in a room,
being cool
feeling bored
teasing one another
gossiping
boys and girls
14 and 15 years old
one boy grabs the hat
of his friend
folds the bill in half
Dude, you nigger-billed my hat!
(The Black kid who just moved from the city
wears his hat bill that way.)
Oh, my bad.
The first boy punches
the second in the arm
lightly
they all laugh
except
the one
brown
girl
in the room

You can't say that.

Oh, no one means you. You're cool.
You can't ever use that word.

You're overreacting!
We're not talking bad about you.
You're not like
other Blacks.

Everyone in the room
in agreement
except
the one
brown
girl.

WELCOME TO THE NEIGHBORHOOD?

The sellers heard a rumor
of culture
so...
the darkest buyers
submitted the highest bid
still...
There is a small delay on the seller's end.

The phone call came unexpectedly.
Please come to the annual street block party.

Everyone was so welcoming
Every single neighbor approached them
jovially
introduced themselves,
pointed out their homes,
their kids
told jokes
complimented one another's dishes
potluck

Your girls are so well-mannered
Oh, you're in upper management?
You already live here in town; just a mile away?
Oh, you're looking to upsize?

I bet you're excited about the prospect of having your very own private pool?

They drove one mile away
silently
feeling the violation
on the tip of their tongues

The sale went through.
They moved in.
Everyone was so friendly.

Almost a year later,
at the mailbox,
she asked about the street block party
potluck

Oh, that was really just a one-time thing.

FAMOUS LAST WORDS

George Floyd couldn't
BREATHE
A 200-pound knee on his neck
a $20 sham
and neither could
Eric Garner
strangled
for no permit
or Manuel Ellis
walking home after church
Michael Brown begged
Stop Shooting Me
Stop Shooting Me
executed
hands up
shots fired
arm
arm
arm
arm
head
head
Six minutes from confrontation
to dead in the street
body lain
on unyielding concrete

more than four hours
his Mama
behind the yellow tape
waiting
watching
wailing
her footsteps colliding into
the same concrete
her son lay atop
hardening
where he'd fallen
captured
steps away
from her
in his own blood
police officers unholstered
guns
killed him
refusing to let her touch her baby
Emmitt Till
fourteen
so beautiful
His mama wanted everyone to see
the ugly
they cut off
his ears
maybe he didn't have to hear
his own screams

Trayvon Martin
fifteen
died with skittles
on his breath
and his acquitted
murderer
gained celebrity
signing bags of skittles
Philando Castile
told the police officer
he had a firearm
I'm not reaching for it
and the cop fired into his car
sitting beside his lady
his baby
girl
behind them
he
died moaning
they could not touch him
could not move
had to just watch
his final exhale
Breonna Taylor
couldn't even get a good night's sleep

The last thing
Ahmaud Arbery

heard
before he died
NIGGER!
Sandra Bland
hung in a jail
cell after a botched
traffic stop
because she talked too much
Tamir Rice
was twelve
years old
playing with an airsoft replica
in a park
no time to talk,
shot within twelve seconds
Tanisha Anderson
in a fitful mental health crisis
her family asking for help,
it came in the form of murder
in the middle of the road
her nightgown hiked up over her hips
her daughter watching from a window
Did you see her one last time,
like that?
Walter Scott
shot dead running
away
after a stop

for a non-functioning brake light
Atatiana Jefferson's neighbor
called the police, worried about her

the police officer shot
her through her bedroom window
while she played video games
with her eight-year-old nephew
Medgar Evers
shot down
in his own driveway
his last words
Turn Me Loose
Martin Luther King Jr's last words
to musician Ben Branch
Play 'Take My Hand, Precious Lord'

Killing us then
Killing us again
and AGAIN
Elijah McClain
played the violin for homeless animals
I just can't breathe
correctly

Part Three: Take My Hand

Precious Lord, Take My Hand
Thomas A. Dorsey (1899 - 1993)

When my way grows drear precious Lord linger near
When my light is almost gone
Hear my cry, hear my call
Hold my hand lest I fall
Take my hand precious Lord, lead me home

Precious Lord, take my hand
Lead me on, let me stand
I'm tired, I'm weak, I'm lone
Through the storm, through the night
Lead me on to the light
Take my hand precious Lord, lead me home

SCRIPTURE

Loving Our Enemies
has been a mortal trial
for the descendants
of Africans
in America.

We tried
patience
prayed
to be treated
as flesh of Your flesh
with plentiful protests
and
the rare insurrection
We delivered
kindness,
raising "white"
children earnestly
while our babies grew up or died
orphans
We submitted
humbly,
not looking "whites" in the eyes
resigned to the back of the bus
this
entire

country
fabricated
on our
mangled
backs,
gratuitously
seasoned
with our vitality
even as those
impersonating
American
countrymen
defiled
us

Little by little we resist
largely on snatched pieces of the dream
and when you see us with full scraps,
dangling from airborne
fists,
bronzed
and overcome
you say,
See
racism is gone
Now
they can just move
on

get over it

In this "white" America
we have mastered
long-suffering

A "white" sister recently implored
me to remember
the unalienable
rights
battle
of African Americans
is not against flesh and blood
"white" people
but against
Satan.

I reminded her
the
standardized
pounding
of
brown flesh
has rerun
since
1619
and
our blood soaks

the soil
asphalt
grass
concrete
hard wood floors
carpets
flower beds
roots
of America

Satan uses
"white"
supremacy as his
noose
bullet in our backs
knee on our necks
blindfold
unjust system
prison cell
foot kicking us when we are down
hell
on earth

Maybe
I told her
It is actually "whites"
fighting the battle
and losing

your souls
to Satan
as you crush ours.
She stared at me, horrified.

What does it mean, Lord,
the last shall be first,
and the first shall be last?

The oldest known human remains
were found in Africa
Eve
We all descend from her
and her husband
created
in Your image

Are we at the bottom of the barrel
now
toiling
naked, hungry,
thirsty
scraping for dignity
because we were
first
right there with You,
in Your flawless garden
and still we were not sated?

Or, are we destined
to be first
in all
eternity
because we toil
here
at the bottom of the barrel
defenseless
famished
parched
scraping
for dignity?

MASS MURDER

The caption read
Miraculous
she'd sent me the video
of family members
of Dylann Roof's nine victims
forgiving him
one by one
at his first appearance
in court

less than forty-eight hours
after they welcomed him into their prayer meeting
and he repaid them with bullets
inside their church

He'd been taken to the hearing
clad in a vest
designed to protect him
from his own mortal sin

I watched the video of arrest
envy teared my eyes
when I saw the police
approach his vehicle
put their guns back in their holsters

They saw a thin
white
male
looking younger
than his 19 years
and reminding them of a quirky
kid they knew and loved

those same eyes perceive
my son as much older
than his years

To me,
Dylann Roof
looked like most mass murderers
white male
he looked
like a white supremacist

It is miraculous,
I scoff when I call her
my fury too lengthy
to text
We forgive
and forgive
and forgive
forgive
forgive

forgive
forgive

When do they get what they deserve?

Her joy
emits from her cell tower
to mine
her grace like carrier oil
even before she opens her mouth

My sister,
And so what?
I think about it
I get angry
Then I ask myself
but, how can we
except
by Him

Who would I rather be?

Resilient,
humble,
forgiving,
obedient to God
no matter what!

Let man do his finite worst

Let His grace
shame them
strike them down
in His time
Let His children be murdered
by man
in His house
and raised to eternal life
by His blood

Let the survivors
Find comfort
in only Him

We are otherworldly

Our rejoicing shall be
infinite

My Sister,
forgiveness is the ultimate
freedom

And, my Sister,
stop saying them,
stop saying they,

stop saying us
stop saying we

IDENTITY

They were both near the bookbags
and she accidentally knocked his water bottle over
with her elbow
and he said,
Pick it up, Slave!
and she did because she had knocked it over
and then she went to the teacher
a nine-year-old
white
male
had spewed venom
she required an antidote
only, the white teacher
treated his words like
a mosquito bite,
she remained defiled
she had to invoke the elders
I could see the question
even before it spilled out
Why do
they think I'm not good
at nine, this was not her first assault
her *good*
swaddled
(smart
beautiful

116

worthy
precious)
she had been made to feel lacking
had been forced to coddle
and to protect
since pre-K,
her formal introduction into
the
wide white world
She couldn't expose
them
didn't have to
I took them on
bundled them
with my own
virtues
still
left
up for debate

But, I know
they are wrong,
she doesn't smile
her eyes
projectors of
steadfast
faith
because God has me seated

up in the heavenly places
with him.

Amen!
I shout at her,
to Him
and my anger
is refurbished
into gratefulness
and
awe
because this child
picked up the water bottle
went to the helper
pursued justice
when it seemed evasive
recognized her worth
in Him,
despite the plans of the Evil One
to extinguish her

In this child
is THE LIGHT
so powerful
it exposes hate
absent
eclipse
her power supply

her view
is
eternal

PLEASE PRAY FOR ME

When I asked you
to pray
because a mutual friend wanted to sit with me
to discuss
the current trend toward racial restoration
and better understand
you decided to pray for me
to hear her
see her
point of view

Oh, God help us
if even our prayer warriors are protecting
the state
of affairs

How do I tell you
Without sounding prideful
I don't need that prayer.

I am adept at seeing things from the viewpoint
of my white sister
a lifetime of her viewpoints
etched into me
subliminally

I need you to pray my full
brown lips will look innocuous enough
my distinct voice
resilient and strong
won't sound resentful
I need you to pray
For God to translate
concepts foreign to her
into heart knowledge
permeate
her mind
transforming
the way she raises her daughter
and interacts with mine

I was hoping you would know
without me telling you

BLACK DOLL

"Ha! Ha! Ha! Ha!
Look at the
little Black
girl with her
little Black
doll.
That's hilarious!"
a milk-skinned tween girl,
long blonde sloppy bun
bright blue eyes
teenie bikini
floating next to her friend
milky skin
long brown ponytail
bright blue eyes
teenie bikini

in the neighborhood pool
pointing across the water
at my cocoa daughter
only three
and a half,
swimming
placidly
with her floatie
and her barbie

oblivious to their malice

"What's so funny about it?"
I demand
They hadn't seen me behind them,
holding my other cocoa
daughter
just an infant
splashing and kicking and gurgling,
enjoying the
chill
the pool offered
on that scorching
Georgia summer
day.

"Well..it's just..I mean…
I've never seen it before…"

"What? A Black girl?
Or a Black doll?"

"Um, a Black Doll"
question mark

"Then you best get out of this pool,
go walk over to your parents,
and tell them you need to be exposed

to the wider world.
Back when you played with dolls,
didn't they look like you?"
She stared
frozen
in the fog of entitlement
"My daughter deserves
the marketing and sale of brown dolls
so she can play with ones
that look like her."

I hawked these words,
willing her to tell her parents
daring her parents to confront me
daring the entire milky pool population
to confront me
I would drown them all

Those girls swam
frantically to the ledge
and climbed out

I scanned the pool and deck for my
children –
one
two
three
and pulled the baby into my chest

the only
four
The five of us outnumbered
by assumptions of whiteness

I took the warrior stance
I deploy
when the white world
advances

My ears rang with phrases
beginning
"We"
&
"They"

And end
"us"
&
"them"

"always"
&
"never"
strewn between

the enemy

continued to compress
to slowly squeeze good
senseless
and slit my heart
empty
of The Blood

But,
the whisper
Marcia

Marcia
was there
with we
terrified
novices
when our eldest child was born,
drying my brow
joking with Hubby
kissing my forehead
at my most wretched
respiring my resolve
when I
imagined I wanted to die

Marcia
loved him even
before he was born

when he was just two
pink lines
and then
a black and white
ultrasound
image

called him her
Babyman

Marcia
learned to spell
his Nigerian
name
and pronounce it -
Ejaife –
age-eye-if-A
her slight southern drawl
gave me the confidence
to go through with giving it to him
even after my next door neighbor
advised he would
…never be President
or get a good job
with a name like that.
{This was before Barack Hussein Obama}
But, of course,
when it came to college admission

...benefit from Affirmative Action...

Marcia
spent an afternoon
helping
me paint his nursery,
doing most of the work
herself
meticulously

And the
three-and-a-half-year-old
with the Black barbie?

Marcia gifted
her very first
dollhouse
on her first
birthday,
she knew to choose
the model with the brown family

It had been a big
deal to me
when I opened the box,
and saw a brown plastic family
smiling and naive
but it had not

been a big deal
to Marcia

Or any deal at all

Marcia,
milky skin
blonde hair
blue eyes
born and raised in Alabama
just knew

every girl is worthy

of playing with dolls
in her image

RACIAL RECONCILIATION IN THE TIME OF CORONAVIRUS

YOU
slayed
us of connection
confidence
carelessness
We clung to
YOU
dripping in fear
offered up
by news
casters
in twenty-four-hour increments
continuously
times seven
on demand
three hundred sixty-five
days
writhed in uncertainty
we prayed
as death tolls
climbed
our agendas deleted
working
schooling
shopping

exercising
partying
all on pause
watching it
from home

we begged for answers
knowing YOU required
some specific action

so
when we saw
the murders
when we discovered
Ahmaud was just out for a run
honestly
and then Amy tried to put a hit
out on Christian,
duplicitous
and we stood holding our breaths
as we watched George
struggle for life
8:46
we couldn't hold
our breaths
for even
a count
of one

YOU
orchestrate all
we were agape

it hit some
of us
like scalding
brine water
on
raw scar tissue

others
were bushwacked
reality having been
safeguarded
behind the overgrowth
of prerogative

Still others,

kept breathing

averted their eyes
satisfied
it's not me,

or snickered
at the absurdity

because Black heroes are warped
While
white heroes are photoshopped

I sat stuck to the couch
eyes crossed
looking
to YOU
and to the media

they showed me
how
YOU
whitewashed the landscape
of resistance
no longer were the soldiers mostly
brown
I saw lighter hues
eyes wide open
angry
like never before
in numbers larger
than ever before
louder

YOU
took a large part
of what we took for granted

away from us
YOU
dimmed
the majority
so when
YOU
illuminated
travesty
we
stood
witness

We sat newly
still
and quiet
bored
while the television
electrocuted

When Ahmaud's
and George's
and Breonna's
and Rayshard's
sweet Elijah's
Countless'
breaths were
stolen
shockwaves

commissioned
us into
PROTEST

All Lives can't matter until Black Lives Matter
Silence is Violence
When George Cried Out for his Mama, it was a battle cry to ALL
MAMAS
We See You. We Hear You.
Racism is a Pandemic too
That's not a chip on my shoulder, it's YOUR KNEE at my neck.
8:46 minutes to kill a Black man, 3 days to arrest a murderer
We are not trying to start a race war.
We are trying to END ONE.
The Black Holocaust 1619 – ?
How Many Weren't Filmed?
We Pay You to Protect Us, Not Kill Us.
I Can't Breathe
ENOUGH!

WHY NOW?

I have asked YOU
why these deaths
these videos
sparked humanity

And all of a sudden
mothers who had previously
remained silent
continued to exchange recipes
and take their sons to little league
and mindlessly swipe
through social media
watched those videos too
their minds blown
they wept
and took up their little
sons in arms

and lined the streets
and shouted
BLACK LIVES MATTER
when three months ago they liked
BLUE LIVES MATTER
and loved
ALL LIVES MATTER

Finally
but YOU still haven't answered
Why Now?

One white woman commented
BETTER LATE THAN NEVER
I could not "like"
wished there was a way to "hate" it
the cartoonish angry
red face
is not enough

BETTER LATE THAN NEVER

can be said when one rushes in disheveled,
tardy
to a dinner party
or when a prodigal son
masters sobriety

Dead Sons
merit
righteous turns
of phrase

There is a time and place for everything under heaven

God will call the past to account

BLESSING

I know your proclivity
is to serve
what you think your fellow
white evangelicals
can eat
without choking

when you pureed
"privilege"
into
"blessing"
it was really just
salted seasoning
meant
to help swallow
acrid
truth
tenderly

it's hidden razors blades
slashed
my trachea
slits
yet unhealed
it continued to descend
collapsed

my lungs

I know
you know
pillage
extermination
annihilation
as handiwork
of the EVIL ONE
and those under
his tutelage
are not blessed

But God
dishes
truth
wrapped
warm
flavored
by His
favor
for those who
sup
with Him

and their children's
children's
children's

children

The fraud
of generational blessing
is actually
generational
pestilence

BLACK FRAGILITY

When you come to me
bashfully
I think I might want to start rapping
It is not me who almost freaks out
but you

when I smirk and reply
Bet,
because I know how much you loathe
my use of your generation's slang
I think you'd be really lit!
You roll relieved eyes
your teenaged exasperation
almost as cute to me as your toddler's jubilation

I don't ask,
What happened to being a surgeon,
with soccer as your backup?

I'm THAT mom,
who requires 100%
Unless you've given 100%
in which case I push you to give
150% next time
With you
all things are possible.

You joke my math isn't great.
Who cares?
as long as yours is exceptional;
I already have my degree.

This is not a moment of me
trying to be cool
now
you're almost sixteen

Trust
when I tell you
I will never
be the cool mom

It's just
I remember
when you wanted
spiky yellow hair
and *pink skin*
you begged
to go by your middle name
because your Nigerian
first name was constantly being mispronounced
made fun of

not even attempted

I remember when you struggled in school;
just one more thing
made you feel outshined
behind
everyone else

I remember seeing your thoughts
and reading
I just want to be white
like everyone else.

I prayed then
God
would help me
disciple you
stand you up tall enough
to look everyone
straight in the eye
speak clearly enough
His Word
would be heard

I prayed your best would hold up
exceedingly
and
abundantly
because, it would have to

I prayed
Daddy and I would model
the beauty of our brown skin
in what we loved
and stood for

God answered

you excel
literally
in
every
single
thing
you pursue

you wear your hair in locs
you look people in the eye
state
your name
in such a way
gives them no other choice
but to try it on
for size

It suits you

your care

144

for what you care for
is meticulous

I had feared
bringing
you up
in a world
where you are one of a few
would create grievance

I should have trusted

my fears
are rendered
fruitless

When I introduced you to Christ
He
told you who you were
and you (mostly) believed Him
no one's perfect

When you tell
me you want to be a rapper
all I see is God
working a miracle
on the little boy
who didn't want to be himself

A babyman
molded
chiseled bronze
a ManChild
beloved
whom God stands for

UnFRIEND

Habitual social media
is a toxic diversion
my entry into the abyss
emotional regurgitation
of friends' friend's friends
has incited
unfriending
like rapid gunfire
what started as a click
here
a click there
now I'm
recklessly
abandoning
old friends
and new

UnFriending
someone I have always
adored

for the comments of her friends
I clicked anyway.

She is not a Christian.

She came to me privately.
She asked what she'd done wrong.

I was dismissive and prideful.

She listened. Digested.
She did not respond.

She appeared at an event I held.
To support me
despite
in the background
I noticed her accidentally

Her love humbling
even as I had so callously thrown her away.

She is not a Christian.
I am.

She allowed me to
ReFriended her.

I marvel at her resemblance to God.

ANXIETY

Honestly,
the part of my heart
settled on home
reluctant to send you
to school
isn't thinking
only about the virus
and the teachers
(God help them)

my heart
is clutching you

third grade
was when three teachers told us they couldn't do
anything
else for your brother
if we weren't going to have him evaluated
and medicated
he was struggling
to focus
to sit still
to perform well on tests

they were done teaching
him after nine weeks

third grade
was the first time your other brother
complained he thought a teacher
had a different set of eyes on him
than the ones she admired
his buddies with

third grade was when your sister
was called
slave
by a classmate

You are rising
up
to third grade

in school you work extra hard,
talking yourself into believing
it will mean you get home sooner

I wonder if the origin
of angst
is your position

seven years
worth of injustices
have been processed
by your youngest

brain
your siblings' accounts of the wide world

here is the safe house
school often
won't be

The pandemic hit
and now you are going
to third grade
and we have to choose
home?
school?
while I wring my hands
indecision
we try to remain separate
but active

at the pool
a little girl
who used to be in your class
informed you
*My Daddy said Black people and white people
are in a war. I don't know if we can play.*

You simply shrugged
*Well, I'm going to play. You can play with me
if you want.*

You relayed the conversation
as a post-
conceived notion

reality smacked my forehead

as soon as we step
out of our house
we dive
into strange mists
of potential
bigotry

but your youngest
brain
has been coached
into a most
competent challenger

MASKED MINORITY

"White"
folks
might have a harder time hearing *no*
they aren't as accustomed
to the craters
it blasts
and hollows out

I tell my kids
No
training them for the world
they orbit
the crushing cold shoulders
floors falling out from under
canyons
they must hurdle

they cannot be gravity-bound

Yours have a smoother surface
to traverse
their legs
don't have
to bound
powerfully
their lungs

153

don't need
increased capacity
yours won't need the practice

restraining resentment
is hard
but we can do
nearly
impossible things

I soak mine
in denial
softening
their futures
so they won't snap
under pressure

Everyone else…
doesn't work in our home
because my kids can't be like
everyone else

Firstly,
because they are His
Secondly,
He made them
darker
and placed them

in this country

I think it's cute
you feel funny
at the grocery store
if there are more people not wearing masks
than people
like you
wearing them

You say it makes you feel like an alien
on an inhospitable planet
Welcome to my world!
I say
it makes me feel like a SuperHero
saving lives
or like the only kid in class
who got an A.

At this, we both laugh
You're messing up the curve!
you tease,
and, I think that's exactly
my purpose

NECESSARY EVIL

sit
your child down
and
say
to your child
we have committed
heinous acts
hand over foot
underhandedly climbed

scapegoats
died
holding us up
the survivors
remain destitute
ignore them
walk away

we write the rules
it is all okay
our house is big
our cars, shiny
our food all non-GMO

sit him down
tell him

he is smarter
more attractive
better in every way

tell him he's to sleep
in that big house
with a gun aimed at
the peasants
ready to shoot
drive the car
eat the food

because of the acts
of the ancestors
even though he is not responsible
for the acts
of his ancestors

it was all unfortunate
it is all over now
but it was necessary
for him to be where he is.

WHITE WOMAN TEARS

C: *Why don't you let one of your white friends handle it?*

She asked me this,
my white Friend,
when I told her
I had agreed
to meet with
another white woman
who was having trouble
understanding
all the racial turmoil

C: *If you don't get through to her you'll have to deal with the
frustration and pain, if you do get through to her you'll have to
deal with white woman tears.*

HA! I laughed out loud.

White woman tears…
the tears
that outrage society
tears
that have been the death
of us
society holds
the sentiment of white women

in the palm of its hand
and wrings the conceptions
of Black women
in lifeless
grips

outrage demands
white women
be harbored

White woman tears
are permissible
and accepted
insomniac
emotional emissions

White woman tears
trump
Black women fears

I thought about my youngest daughter
who had a shadow
following her in first grade
a girl that constantly invaded her space
and when she would say
on my advice
Please, leave me alone.
the girl would cry

And, my daughter would be terrified
What if the teacher thinks I'm being mean?
But you are NOT being mean.
What if she doesn't believe me?
Just tell the truth.
What if I get in trouble?
I will defend you.
Because she knew already
at six
that when a white girl loses tears
reparations must be paid

The white woman
requesting
comprehension
did not cry
she yo-yoed
indignant
suspicious
flippant
I sat on the other end of the phone wishing
she would just cry already

Which is why when you called me
to apologize
for something you said
that hurt me

you cried
I
did not roll my eyes

White Woman Tears
here
are emphatically
empathetic

I did that
I brought on those tears
and I felt equal parts
sorrow
because I have come to know
and love you,
and
relief
you
can see the tiny part of you
inside the you
you want to be
that held hidden
inclinations
you are able to regret

Your
I'm sorry
your tears

were met with my
Thank you
Thank you
for seeing me
and seeing yourself
and hearing me
and hearing yourself

I am aware that you are not required to

You could go through your entire life
successfully
and never
be gotten through to

I shouldn't have to thank you for this

Thank you

ACTS 17: 27, 28

The lunge I
extended
toward Him,
arms outstretched,
waving blindly
grasping
gasping
then, forgetting
rewound
letting go
ignoring
then, remembering
needing
again
a step toward Him again
pushed and pulled
sometimes simultaneously
by trust
or by sin
desperate
for my own power
starved for His
the same distance
the same arrogance
all that is required
a reaching out

an infinitesimal
step forward
deliverance
for the racist
too
that step
those steps
only
everything
that separate
the racist
from Him
too

Jeremiah 29:12-14

We
all
hear
His preface
the plans He has for us
are good
to frame our future
custom make our aspirations
we believe Him
jump up
and run toward our fortunes
the ensuing
murmurations
follow us
inaudible by choice
we don't hear
we must pray
He will listen
we must search for Him
with pliable hearts
He will free us
restore what was stolen
collect us
return us to our
Homeland
we run

Joiya Morrison-Efemini

too quickly
too far away
to hear
his courting whispers
too matchless
for our corrupted ears

THE GENTLEMAN

When you have plummeted
to the bottom of the well
with your kids
you whisper up at them

when you told me this
I laughed
over my laugh you said
It works!

My kids don't hear me
unless my eyes are popping out of my head
while my neck muscles strain
the sound leaving my mouth
so destructive
it would blast the brick
of any well
and drown everyone inside in boiling water

Then I tried it
I whispered
robustly
and with the children's attention,
God got mine
it is exactly
how He deals with us

Satan bulldozes
but God
simply
breathes

"Let the White People Die"

is what you heard

When you asked me
If I had been taking my kids out
attending the protests
And I said,
I'm afraid of the virus
and also for my kids
some lunatic
white supremacist
could decide to shoot
or run us over with his car
Let the white people go out
I said
and you heard:
Let your children
be gunned down
run over
in the street

Your children
are worth
less

You remained silent
and I interpreted that silence

as judgment
I heard you saying
Coward! You can post
your feelings
on FB
but you will not take up post
outside
in the street
rallying
in person

Later,
when I confronted you

(I
confronted
you)

asked you why
you remained silent
you told me

My words
Let the white people…
struck you
automatically
like bullet spray
like a twenty ton

paving roller
razing
the people you love most

It was my turn to be silent
was my turn to listen
my turn to apologize
turned from offended
to thoughtless
offender

PINKY PROMISE

Even mamas
pinky promise
our vows stretching out toward
one another
intertwined
tugging
delighting in discomfort
breathing all the way
through to the absence of lack

You were a joy-filled
acquaintance
but you parked
your car equipped with the sign
you'd held
in another protest
on another day
anonymously
you walked up the hill
to meet us
on a busy corner
in our small, white town
your mouth said
I STAND WITH YOU
your eyes
could not hide the pain

in undeniability
your heart too big
not to stop
when you saw my son
as I see him
then you saw me
and yourself
meeting me
and the many sons
and daughters
no longer able to stand
where we were –
outnumbered and exhausted -
you became a joy-filled Friend

Your art is triumphant
varnished brushstrokes
in His likeness,
founded
on His blessings
so you must disavow
colorblindness
you know every hue He created is good
you attempt to mix them into the visions
materializing
in your head
like our hands
trained for battle

connected at their weakest
extremities fearfully
and wonderfully matched
unshaken
it is first nature
for you to memorialize light
for this fallen world

Here a pinky swear risks amputation
but we are foreigners
set apart together
sealed supernaturally
grace guides us
to put away childish things
our purest promises
deliberately
break historical bonds
miraculously
create everlasting ones

Our work
is to be better to the infinite power
to abide in the Excellence
that turns worlds right
side up
to post a love covenant
and to go viral

BOTANICAL

Your flower
is the Bird
of Paradise
marvelous arms
outstretched
thin and sharp
on the surface
and
graceful feet
pre-
or post-
leap
acrobatic

when we perused
the Botanical Gardens
you climbed everything,
climbable
grand jetéd your way
through whimsically trimmed
shrubbery
your dexterous arms
spanned the whole
wide
world

we breezed through the other exhibits
but when we entered the exotics
greenhouse,
you reached
your hand callow
skyward into mine
one hundred
butterflies
danced
to fountain
instrumentals
contracting bodies
twisting
wings in slanted
figure eights

in a flutter
we were surrounded
by gregarious children
akin
your genus
magnificence
strokes of
apricot
apple
concord
lemon
long, lean lines

purposed toward heaven

this was not your course
you are used to being the foreign
flower
in a bed of roses
breezes blown too freely
swinging you capriciously
into thorns

your hearty roots
guarantee a perennial bloom
regardless of where you've been sown

large leaves
offer fan-like
asylum

even
still,
there among your cohort
I saw your flourish

you released my hand
I took one step back
then six more

you weaved yourself into their festoon

clothed in the same shirt,
in varying sizes
identifying each of them as members of a whole
you fit
cloaked
as you are in petals
indistinguishable

I saw your face photosynthesize
here unadulterated
your pigmentation elemental

I was happy to allow
you taste
the sweet nectar
of self sameness
aromatic rapture
excited sunbirds draw
bask
bathe
pollinate
the propagation of pride
by virtue of sanguinity

I remained seven steps behind
as they
waved off
backward

Your eyes chased them
romanticized
the place
they journeyed from

you'd like to be uprooted
replanted
wearing that shirt

The wind blustered
in their wake
for a moment
you were blind to the butterflies
deaf to the fountain
the colors within
the greenhouse
greyed

You are hardy
do not wilt
do not wither

Took seven steps
toward me,
squeezed my hand
you led
and climbed
grand jetéd

to the exit

It is enough
to know the plots of roses
are not the most excellent

there is a time and place
their thorns won't exist

Acknowledgments

First and foremost, I thank **my Lord and Savior Jesus Christ** for the gifts He so graciously bestows upon me, and for the opportunities He gives me to share them.

There are so many people to thank for this work. So many I fear I may forget someone. If I do, I ask for grace. I thank my beloved editor of PETRIFIED FLOWERS, **Lisa Dunn**, who saw a few of these poems on FB and encouraged me to write an entire collection. Thank you, **Anne M. Kaylor**, for choosing *Comfortable Walk* to appear in moonShine Review. I thank my amazing writing group – **Anna Prineas Catanese, Jennifer Graham Kizer, Kirsten Gant, and Renee Lichtenhen** - for all the time you dedicate to reading my hastily typed words - typos and all - and your sharp eyes as you muddle through, making my words more powerful. Thank you to my unofficial reader, **Karen Saboura**. You always read every single word generously and pour out gentle honesty and wisdom with every suggestion. I thank **Kennedy Champitto** and **Sarah Caro** for loving this collection enough to publish it under their imprint. I thank every single person who inspired a poem, most notably, **Dad and Mom**; **Kelly Marcuzzi**, my Friend, you humble me in your belief that my poems are worthy amongst some of the most poignant in history; **Carol Ogle**; **Marcia Paul**; **Chris Disser**; my Sissy, **Nicole Johnson** whose BLACK is so BEAUTIFUL; **Laurie O'Connor**, who views everything always from the perspective of eternity; **Renata McCreary**; **Corinne Mitchell**; **Eki Ehigiamusoe** for praying the accusations "THEY" and "THEM" out of my vocabulary; **Edugie Asemota**; and **Frannie Vookles**, who whispers.

I am ever grateful to my children and to my husband, **Efe**.

Joiya Morrison-Efemini is the author of three previous works, all written in verse – THE NOTES THEY PLAYED (2017), THE IMPOSSIBLE (2019), PETRIFIFED FLOWERS (2020). She lives in Marietta, Georgia with her hunky husband, four phenomenal children, a dog named Deuce and a cat named Gia.

Printed in the USA
CPSIA information can be obtained
at www.ICGtesting.com
BVHW032148250823
668878BV00001B/30